Land

WEATHER

Troll Associates

WEATHER

by Louis Sabin

Illustrated by Joseph Veno

Troll Associates

Library of Congress Cataloging in Publication Data

Sabin, Louis.
    Weather.

    Summary: Explains how day-to-day variations in the
weather are determined by the interrelationships among
temperature, humidity, wind, and air pressure.
    1. Weather—Juvenile literature. [1. Weather]
I. Veno, Joseph, ill. II. Title.
QC981.3.S23   1984   551.5   84-2706
ISBN 0-8167-0200-4 (lib. bdg.)
ISBN 0-8167-0201-2 (pbk.)

One summer morning the sky is a bright, clear blue. The sun is shining and the air is hot. As the day goes on, clouds begin to drift through the sky, blocking the bright rays of sunshine. The wind whips through tree leaves, and the air turns chilly. The sky darkens and a sudden flash of lightning blazes a jagged path across the sky. Rain pours down, soaking the dry ground. Then the rain stops and, as evening falls, the sky is clear again, and the air is sweet and cool.

Every year brings us warm days and cold days, wet days and dry days, heavy snows and gentle rains. When it is warm we wear thin clothing, and when it is cold we wear heavy clothing. When too much rain falls, there are terrible floods. When there is too little rain, farm crops die. Weather affects us in many ways.

But what is weather? Weather is what happens in the air all around us from day to day. Weather is different from climate. Climate describes the average weather in one place over a long period of time. For example, suppose you live in the southwestern United States, and suppose it is raining today. Today's *weather* where you live would be called wet. But it does not rain very often in your part of the country, so the *climate* where you live is said to be dry.

The main elements of weather are how hot or cold it is; how wet or dry it is; how much wind there is; and what the air pressure is. The way these elements work together gives us our weather.

All our weather begins with the sun. The sun's rays warm the air. Warm air rises, and cool air rushes in to fill the space left by the rising warm air. This movement of cool air and warm air is called wind.

Cool air

Cool air is heavier than warm air. So a large mass of cool air pushes down with great pressure. This mass of cool air is called a *high-pressure system*, or a *high*. A high-pressure system usually brings nice weather, with clear skies.

Warm air pushes down with less pressure than cool air. So a mass of warm air is called a *low-pressure system*, or a *low*. A low-pressure system often brings cloudy skies and storms.

Warm air

Besides heating the air, the sun also heats the surface of the water that fills the oceans, lakes, and rivers on the Earth. The water *evaporates*—it turns into a gas called water vapor. This invisible moisture floats in the warm air. Sometimes it is called humidity. When there's not too much moisture or water vapor in the air, we say that the humidity is low. When there's a lot of water vapor in the air, we say that the humidity is high, and the air may feel moist and sticky.

Water vapor condenses back into water droplets when the temperature of the air reaches the dew point. The dew point is the temperature at which air cannot hold any more water in the form of water vapor. The vapor may condense into tiny water droplets that hang in the air and drift on air currents. This is called fog. Fog forms when warm, moist air blows over cool land or water, or when heat rises from warm ground or water into cool air.

Sometimes water vapor settles on the ground as dew or frost. Dew forms when ground temperature is above freezing. If the temperature is below freezing, frost forms instead of dew. When water vapor rises higher into the air before it condenses into droplets, clouds are formed. There are several different kinds of clouds.

Cumulus clouds are fat and fluffy at the top and gray at the bottom. They are also called fair-weather clouds because they're present on warm, sunny days.

Cool air

Warm air

Sometimes these fair-weather clouds turn into storm clouds called thunderheads. Thunderheads, or cumulonimbus clouds, occur when cumulus clouds rise through warm air until they reach the cool upper atmosphere. This causes the water droplets to condense quickly and fall as rain. If the upper air is very cold, the droplets may freeze and fall to Earth as pieces of ice called hailstones.

Low, flat clouds are called stratus clouds.
They look like a gray blanket in the sky, and
they block out the sunshine.

Rain Sleet Snow
Air in clouds below freezing

Warm air Air below freezing

Clouds that cover the sky on very rainy days are nimbostratus clouds. They usually are thick, dark, and low, and hang overhead like a heavy, wet blanket. When the temperature of the air *under* the nimbostratus clouds is below freezing, the falling rain turns to bits of ice called sleet. When the temperature of the air *in* the clouds is below freezing, the moisture falls as snow.

Cirrus clouds are high-level clouds that look like feathery white plumes. These fair-weather clouds are driven swiftly across the sky by fast winds.

The winds that blow the clouds through the sky bring us our weather. They are named for the direction that they come from. So a north wind is a wind that comes from the north.

Winds may also be classified according to their speed. A wind that barely rustles tree leaves is called a light breeze. A wind that makes tree branches sway is called a strong breeze. A wind that breaks the twigs off trees is called a fresh gale. If the wind can uproot trees, it is called a whole gale. And stronger winds are called either storms or hurricanes.

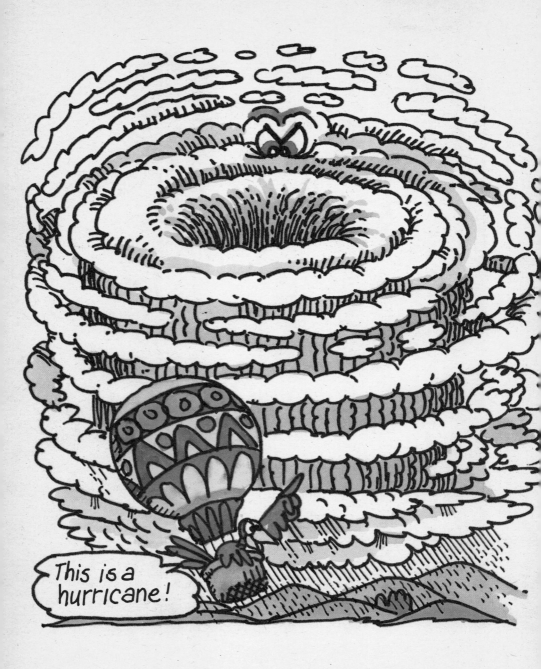

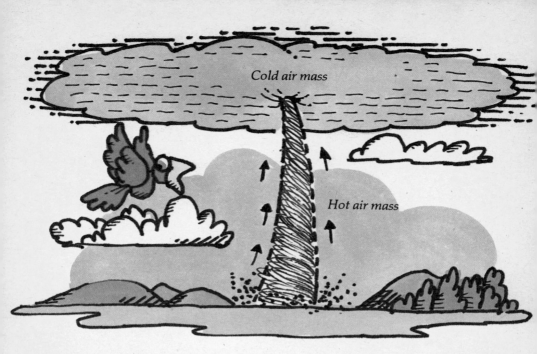

Cold air mass

Hot air mass

Hurricanes—also known as typhoons and cyclones—can destroy houses, crops, and everything else in their paths. A close relative of the hurricane is the tornado. Although tornadoes, also called twisters, do not last very long, they rip a path of destruction across the land. Tornadoes form when a mass of hot air tries to rise through a mass of cold air. The cold mass presses down, and the hot mass presses up. When the hot mass of air finds a hole in the cold mass of air, it rushes through and forms the powerful spinning wind called a tornado.

Warm and cold air masses are always moving in our atmosphere. The places where they meet are called fronts. If the warm air mass is stronger and pushes back the cold air mass, it is called a warm front. If the cold air mass is stronger, it is called a cold front. Air fronts are like battle lines where two forces struggle. The result is bad weather—rain, snow, high winds, thunder, and lightning.

People have always tried to predict the weather so they would know such things as when to plant and harvest crops, when to go on vacation, and when to hold outdoor activities. But until science developed weather-predicting tools, people had to rely on memory of past years, the calendar, and guesswork.

Then, more than 300 years ago, an Italian scientist invented the barometer. The barometer measured the pressure of the air. By watching changes in air pressure, people could get an idea of what the weather was going to be. If the air pressure was rising, there would probably be good weather. If it was falling, the weather would probably be bad. Weather forecasting became a bit more accurate after the telegraph was invented. Information could then be quickly sent across the country.

Meteorologists—scientists who study the weather and its causes—could chart the weather over large regions. With other advances in communications, they could even begin to understand weather patterns all over the world. Balloonists and airplane pilots also supplied information to early meteorologists.

Today, weather forecasting uses a large number of techniques and instruments. There are anemometers to measure wind speed, hygrometers to measure the amount of water in the air, barometers to measure air pressure, rain gauges to measure rainfall, and thermographs to measure and record air temperature.

Telecommunications link weather stations all over the world. Satellites orbit the Earth far out in space, sending back a steady flow of pictures and other information. All of these facts and pictures are fed into electronic computers. And when all of that information is studied, it comes out as a weather report— perhaps the very one you will hear on radio or television tomorrow morning!